AROUND TOWN

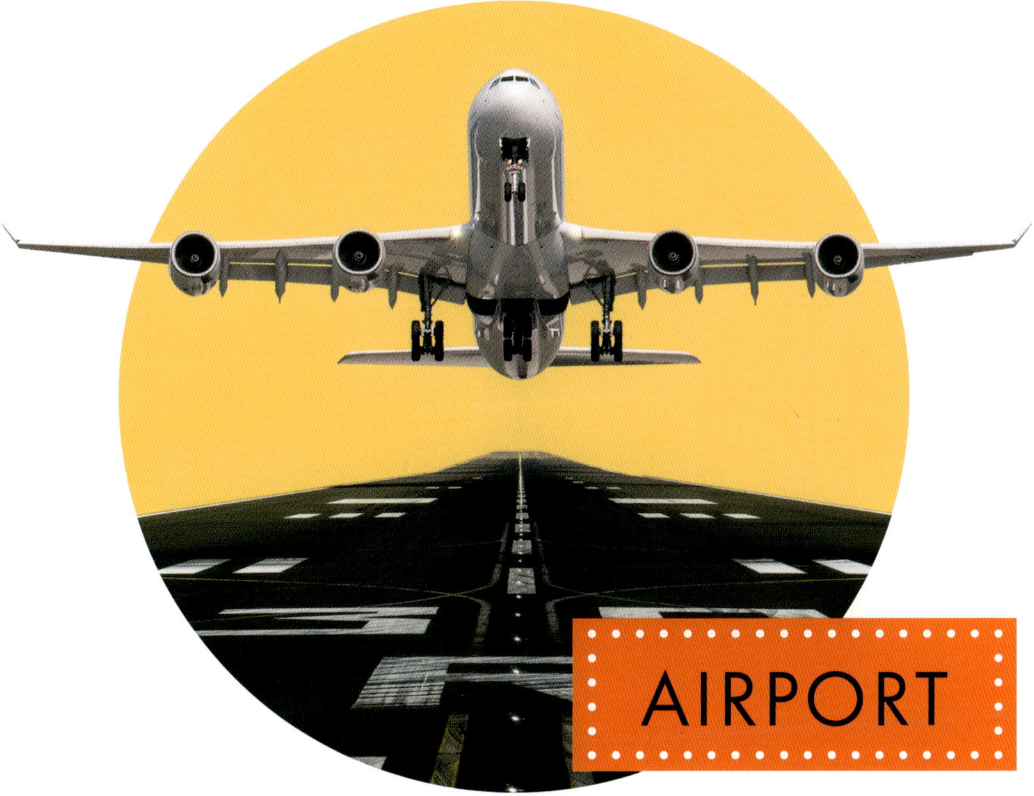

AIRPORT

by Alissa Thielges

security gate

carousel

Look for these words and pictures as you read.

runway

boarding gate

Ready to fly?
Let's head to the airport!

Carl's Jr.

An airport is big.
Planes come and go.
You can eat and shop.

security gate

Look at the security gate.
You step through a machine.
A guard looks for weapons.
It is all safe!

EXIT
Gate 103
Lufthansa
Flug/Flight
LH 858
Code share
SK 3620
Zeit/Time
17:00
nach - über/to - via
Oslo-Gardermoen

boarding gate

Look at the boarding gate.
The plane stops here.
You can get on.

runway

Look at the runway.
Planes take off. They land.
They need a lot of space.

carousel

Look at the carousel.
Bags come off the plane.
You can grab your bag.

Planes go to far places.
It is fun to fly!

security gate

carousel

Did you find?

runway

boarding gate

Spot is published by Amicus Learning, an imprint of Amicus
P.O. Box 227, Mankato, MN 56002
www.amicuspublishing.us

Library of Congress Cataloging-in-Publication Data
Names: Thielges, Alissa, 1995- author.
Title: Airports / by Alissa Thielges.
Description: Mankato : Amicus Learning, [2024] | Series: Spot around town | Audience: Ages 4–7 | Audience: Grades K–1 | Summary: "A search-and-find book about airports reinforces new vocabulary to build reading success while close-up images captivate young audiences. A great early social studies book to inspire learning about communities on field trips for kindergartners and first graders"—Provided by publisher.
Identifiers: LCCN 2023039308 (print) | LCCN 2023039309 (ebook) | ISBN 9781645497318 (library binding) | ISBN 9781645497394 (pdf)
Subjects: LCSH: Airports—Juvenile literature.
Classification: LCC TL725.15 .T45 2024 (print) | LCC TL725.15 (ebook) | DDC 387.7/36—dc23/eng/20231107
LC record available at https://lccn.loc.gov/2023039308
LC ebook record available at https://lccn.loc.gov/2023039309

Printed in China

Rebecca Glaser, editor
Deb Miner, series designer
Kim Pfeffer, book designer and photo researcher

Photos by AdobeStock/think4photop, 8–9; Alamy/Wavebreakmedia Ltd UC24, 6–7; Dreamstime/Christian Heinz, 8, Dezzor, 10–11, Lee Avison, 12–13, Lukas Gojda, 1; iStock/aapsky, 14, buzbuzzer, 3; Shutterstock/chuyuss, cover, Ewa Studio, 4–5